To

_____

On the Occasion of

_____

From

_____

FAITH DANCING

Conversations in good company

JILL BRISCOE

MONARCH
BOOKS

Oxford, UK & Grand Rapids, Michigan

Published in association with the literary agency of Alive Communications, Inc.,
7680 Goddard Street, Suite 200, Colorado Springs, CO 80920.
www.alivecommunications.com

First published in the UK in 2009 by Monarch Books
(a publishing imprint of Lion Hudson plc),
Jordan Hill Road, Oxford, OX2 8DR.
Tel: +44 (0) 1865 302750   Fax: +44 (0) 1865 302757
Email: monarch@lionhudson.com   www.lionhudson.com

Distributed by:
UK: Marston Book Services Ltd, PO Box 269, Abingdon, Oxon OX14 4YN.
USA: Kregel Publications, PO Box 2607, Grand Rapids, Michigan 49501.

ISBN: 978-1-85424-883-1 (UK)
ISBN: 978-0-8254-6288-7 (USA)

Photos: L. Alexander, R. Chouler, J. Crawford, S. Dicks, E. Lobban,
A. Rogers, N. White, K. Smith.

British Library Cataloguing Data
A catalogue record for this book is available from the British Library.

Printed and bound in China.

DEDICATED TO THE NEXT GENERATION
OF YOUNG PEOPLE WHO, WITH JOY AND
COMMITMENT,
WILL FINISH THE JOB JESUS GAVE US
TO DO 2000 YEARS AGO. THE FUTURE OF
CHURCH AND
MISSION IS IN GOOD HANDS. MAY EACH
OF YOU CARE WELL FOR YOUR OWN SOUL
SO THAT GOD CAN USE YOU TO CARE
WELL FOR OTHERS.

CONTENTS

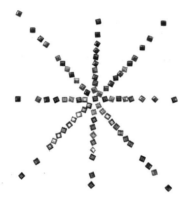

FAITH DANCING

INTRODUCTION

Sometimes our faith is tired. It seems to have nowhere to sit down and have a rest. It's hard to hope for better things and we need a helping hand. It is at such times I go to the Deep Place where nobody goes, sit on the Steps of my Soul and breathe deeply. Through His Word help comes. Strengthened by such encounters I continue. Not just plodding, hanging on with grim determination to finish the course set before me, but with renewed joy – my faith dancing. My prayer is that this little book would encourage your faith to sit down and have a rest too. Enjoy!

Jill Briscoe

FAITH DANCES

A misty moment in the dawn
When faith returns and hope is born,
Where shadowed by God's present-ness
I celebrate and so confess
My doubt and fear,
My sins leave here,
Faith dances.

Why wait I till my broken soul
Despairs of ever being made whole
And I can't see why Christ who died
For all my sins was crucified?
Restore my sight,
My Lord, my Light,
Faith dances.

So deep inside I find Your peace,
A final spiritual release,
My spirit calms, my heart stands tall,
Renewed, refreshed, I hear Your call.
I will believe,
Your joy receive,
Faith dances!

LIFE LESSONS

"Teach us to number our days aright, that we may gain a
heart of wisdom."
Psalm 90:12

———————— ❧ ————————

I was sitting in the Garden of Grace outside God's
Front Door. Someone had asked me to talk to a church group
about some of my "life lessons".

"That's what happens when you get old," I complained to
the Lord. "People ask you what you'd do differently looking
back on your *'lo-o-ong life'* or some such thing!"

"Well what *are* some of your life lessons, Jill?" He asked
mildly, without assuring me the question was not really
appropriate.

After a talk He left for a while and I lingered, thinking about
His question.

All I could think of were some verses in the Golden Book
that said, "You are not your own, you are bought with a
price."

I thought of His unconditional love towards me and knew

that I had learned and must still learn to be unconditional in my response and the demands I make of God in my service for Him. So I wrote in my journal where I write important things down in case I forget them (you do, you know, when you get along in years and are asked to share your life lessons): "My submission to God must be unconditional."

For example, the words of God to Jeremiah, "You must go to everyone I send you to and say whatever I command you." (Jeremiah 1:7)

Jeremiah was very young and so he said to God, "I am only a child. Wait till I get a bit older, God!" Similarly, when God told Moses what He wanted him to do, Moses said, "Here I am, Lord, but I'm not eloquent. Please send my brother!" Of course, these weren't really conditions but rather refusals!

If I am asked to do something and if I am able to do it, I say "yes". I must not say, "if they pay my way" or "if they will sell my books and CDs" or "if I only speak and don't have to make myself available to the people afterwards". Or "if I can stay in a hotel instead of someone's home – even if it saves you money". No "ifs" or "buts".

My unselfconscious impact on others will be commensurate with the measure that I am given over to serve them and "as much as I do it to one of these, I do it unto Him". *The fragrance of the aroma of Christ is least sensed by those who scatter the perfume of His presence abroad.* I have learned to be content that He knows this is what I am about, whether others know it or not.

Did I say what He told me to say in the power of the Spirit or did I get in the way? How I am received or perceived by others is none of my business. How I am perceived by Him is all that matters to me. I am to live only unto Him.

"Well," I said loudly, "that will do for a start," and I returned from the Garden of Grace and my time with the Lord to face a pile of emails asking me to speak at this, that and the other. I like to think that it was my time in the Garden with Him that determined my ready response.

Dear Lord, You gave your life on earth unconditionally to people for Your Father's sake. And You have told me "as much as you have done it to the least of these you have done it to me". Don't let me pick and choose — You pick and choose for me! Give me insight to know who to serve — when, where, and how. For Your sake Lord, not mine.

For Your sake!

Amen

YES

Yes in today, to Your word,
I heard,
Deep in my mind
About lost mankind,
Yes in these hours
With all of my powers,
Yes, Lord. Yes, Lord, yes!

Yes, to the trouble I'll meet
In the street,
Out and about
Learning to shout
Loudly and clear,
Even in fear,
About You, Lord. Oh yes, Lord, yes!

Yes to the brothers and sisters
Together,
Hearts and minds one
Whatever the weather.
Yes, to the team and our holy endeavour,
Yes Lord. Oh yes Lord, yes!

Yes to Your heart for the lost and the lonely,
Yes to the cost,
Yes to You only.
Yes to Your will: so abide with me still –
Yes, Lord. Yes, Lord, yes!

Yes to Your call about "leaving and
Cleaving",
Yes to your Spirit
I now am receiving,
Yes to the power of faith and believing,
Yes, Lord. Yes, Lord, yes!

FAITH DANCING

YOU MUSTN'T MIND

"FOR THE JOY THAT WAS SET BEFORE HIM, [HE] ENDURED THE
CROSS, SCORNING ITS SHAME."

Hebrews 12:2

We had been with missionaries in a distant and dangerous land.
Some had their children with them. Many had not. They had left
all they loved behind for the sake of the gospel. Christmas was
coming; but their loved ones were not. That was so hard! I spent
time praying for them as my plane sped away so that I could be
with *my* loved ones for Christmas!

I remembered a woman saying to me once, when we were
full-time Christian workers and separated from our family at
Christmas, "You mustn't mind! I could never do that. I love
my husband too much. We've never been apart since we got
married. I could never be separated from him at Christmas."

My lonely heart cried, "I mustn't mind? You love your
husband too much? Do you know how much I love mine?"
But even as I opened my mouth, I heard a voice closer than
breathing, nearer than hands and feet!

"For the joy set before me I endured the cross scorning
its shame," He said. And, I realized, He didn't only endure the

cross but the crib as well! It took thirty-three Christmases before He went home! Imagine… I tried not to resent the woman's remarks as she went on to tell me that she "didn't believe God would bring Christian people together to separate them".

"Sometimes you have no choice," I replied defensively.

"Everyone has a choice," she replied, looking at me severely. I saw my words had no meaning to her. And in a way she was right. Everyone does have a choice. We had made ours, Stuart and I, fifty years ago on our wedding day! "As for me and my household, we will serve the Lord." This choice to follow His call will, for many, mean a very personal cost, yet a small price compared to the one He paid for us. So, for the joy set before us, we endure!

Later we talked, He and I. We talked about the young families out in isolated and difficult places, their "heart hunger" for those they loved so dearly almost too hard to handle.

"One of the hardest things is being apart from family, Lord. It never seems to get any easier."

"Yes."

"Especially at Christmas!"

"I know."

I looked at Him. Of course He knew! Then, "Oh dear Lord! *Thank you!*"

"Thank *you!*" He said, smiling at me. Do you know what that was worth? He blessed me then and gave me His joy. He promised you know!

No joy without Jesus, no happiness deep,
No rest of the soul that gives life-giving sleep,
No freedom from fear that cripples my day,
No joy without Jesus, no peace come what may!

It was pleasing His Father that caused Him to come,
To leave all His angels, His glory, His home,
For the joy set before Him, enduring the cross
He accepted for me all the pain and the loss.

No heart for the lonely who long for a friend?
No plans but to live for myself till the end?
No way would I choose to ignore those who're lost
No matter the hurt, no matter the cost...

It's the joy that's in Jesus that powers my heart
When at times He requires some time far apart,
He came from His Father, a small baby boy,
And He lived and He died to give me His joy.

No strength without Him who gives power to the faint,
No will to endure that He grants to the saints,
No lightness of spirit, no smile on my face,
No joy without Jesus: amazing His grace!

YOU MUSTN'T MIND

This Christmas, pause as a family

and pray for your missionaries

separated for His sake from those they dearly love!

FAITH DANCING

GRUDGES

⁓ ❧ ⁓

*T*WAS SITTING QUIETLY IN THE GARDEN OF GRACE reading from the book of Exodus in the Old Testament. I came to the chapters about the Lord's encounter with Moses in the desert:

" 'What is that in your hand?'

'A staff,' Moses replied.

The Lord said, 'Throw it on the ground.'

Moses threw it on the ground and it became a snake and he ran from it." (Exodus 4:2, 3.)

If you don't deal with a grudge it will turn into a poisonous snake.

I heard Him clearly. I was struggling with holding onto a grudge. A grudge arising from a hurt done to me that I didn't deserve. God was telling me that if I didn't let it go the snake would bite me!

"Lay it down, Moses," God commanded, speaking to Moses "face to face as a man with his friend". "Lay it down!"

FAITH DANCING

God knew there was a snake in the seemingly benign-looking rod! That rod represented Moses' work for God. But you can't do work for God while you're holding on to a grudge. He had to throw it down in order for God to take the snake out of it. Then he could take up his work again and use it for God.

In my book of remembrances I always take with me to the Garden of Grace, I wrote:

> Don't hold onto a grudge – there's a snake in it.
> Don't try to play God. Let God deal with the horrible thing.
> Do my part not theirs. Have I forgiven them? I'm only responsible for my attitude and reaction, not the other person's.

"Throw it down, Jill."

So I did! God dealt with the snake and some time later I heard Him say, "Take it to you again."

Hey, don't try to do the work of God if you're holding onto a grudge. Let it go. Throw it down.

Sit still. Think about this. Are you ready? Tell Him.

GRUDGES

DON'T JUST STAND THERE: DO SOMETHING!

"THOSE WHO HOPE IN THE LORD WILL RENEW THEIR STRENGTH."
Isaiah 40:31

THERE IS A RHYTHM TO LIFE. Work and wait, work and wait. There must be both working and waiting! So often we emphasize one or the other, being critical of those who do all the work and no waiting, or all the waiting but no working! Those who wait on the Lord will renew their strength *in order to do* the working. "They will soar on wings like eagles; they will run and not grow weary, they will walk and not be faint." There is a rhythm to life.

I have a habit of reading first an Old Testament passage and then a New Testament one each day. Early one morning, I read Isaiah 40, followed by the story of the ascension of Jesus in the Acts of the Apostles. So often the scriptures in Old and New Testament both complement and supplement each other. After Jesus had given the men his orders to "wait" till they had been given the power to "work", He was "taken up before their very eyes, and a cloud hid Him from their sight." (Acts 1:9.) I read how the men "were looking intently up into the sky as He was going"; I would think so – what an incredible worship experience. Then suddenly, two men dressed in white stood beside them and said, *"Don't just stand here; do something!"* They assured the men that this same Jesus would come back from heaven as they had seen Him go into heaven, and there was a lot of waiting and a lot of working to do before it would happen! We talked about this, He and I.

"Lord, it must have been incredible to just stand there and watch You ascend into heaven!" But then the angel said to your disciples, 'Don't just stand there; DO SOMETHING!' I like that!"

"Why do you like that?"

"Because I would have done the same thing as your disciples. Just want to spend the rest of my life gazing up into heaven — hoping I'd live to see you come back in the same manner I'd watched you go! I wouldn't have got anything done."

"There's much to do for me yet, Jill. Keep yourself busy till I come!"

"I will, Lord."

"Wait first, and then work — there is a rhythm to life."

Lord, help me keep the balance of work and worship.

Help me to work at worship and then worship as I work.

Amen

DON'T JUST STAND THERE: DO SOMETHING!

SAGE WISDOM

"Now, O Lord my God, you have made your servant king in place of my father David. But I am only a little child and do not know how to carry out my duties... So give your servant a discerning heart to govern your people and to distinguish between right and wrong. For who is able to govern this great people of yours?"

1 Kings 3:7, 9

FAITH DANCING

Have you wondered what to say
Or what to do throughout the day,
When faced with children wild and strong
To give advice on right or wrong?
Do you, like me, need wisdom's light
To pierce a dark dilemma's night?

When Solomon had had a dream
And God had come, or so it seemed,
And offered him a choice so rare,
And told him not to dare despair,
When overwhelmed by life's demands
To give his way into God's hands.

The Spirit's wisdom can be ours
When running out of human powers.
However young, however old,
He'll give you words and you'll be bold
To speak God's wisdom like the Sage,
To benefit your day and age!

SAGE WISDOM

PUT IT IN MY BACKPACK

TUART AND I WERE BIRDWATCHING in Wisconsin – one of our favourite things to do. We were taking a few days to celebrate my birthday (yes, I actually still have them once a year!) walking the trails in the beautiful forests of our state. That morning Stuart had shouldered his backpack loaded with water bottles, maps, bird books, camera, and so on, but I decided to carry just my binoculars and camera and no extra weight. We set off on a glorious morning and oh, oh, oh, what a thrill to be alone with each other and with God and His incredible finger work – and walk and walk and walk. Joy!

"It's so beautiful, Lord, I see You everywhere," I said quietly. "Thank you!" And I remembered it said in the Golden Book: "The invisible things of Him are clearly seen… in the things… [He] made."

After lunch we set off again, and this time the trail was more

isolated and hilly. By now I had accumulated a few items along the way and my hands were full. (Don't ask me "what things" – you know how we women do that – even in the middle of a forest!) The heavy binoculars got heavier still and the "stuff" in my hands more cumbersome. Added to that we were walking uphill. I was dragging.

I walked behind my man and looked at his strong, straight shoulders ahead of me carrying his burden lightly, though his backpack was quite full. Suddenly as if sensing my fatigue, he turned around, smiled at me and said gently, "Jill, put it in my

PUT IT IN MY BACKPACK

backpack." So I took all my stuff and put it in his backpack and we continued to walk the trails. What a relief. What a difference. But my joy was tempered with sorrow.

Stuart turned around to lead up the trail again, and in that moment standing quite still, I acknowledged that as well as all the paraphernalia of the birder I had been carrying another unseen burden of worry that day. A burden that was spoiling the day and casting a shadow over everything. True, my hands were empty but my heart was still loaded down with worry – my spirit still dragging up the hills.

"Why don't you put it in 'My' backpack, Jill?" the Lord whispered to my heavy heart. And there, walking along that beautiful Wisconsin trail I did just that! It didn't mean I didn't have a burden any more. It meant that He was carrying it instead of me: just as Stuart was carrying all my earthly things. What a difference! The problem hadn't gone anywhere, but His strong eternal shoulders were bearing the weight of it. My spirit breathed more easily and my soul relaxed.

"Joy is faith dancing. Peace is faith resting," I heard Him say.

Tell me, are you walking the forest trails of life with a heavy weight on your heart? A worry so grievous it's crushing you and spoiling the day? Put it in His backpack! Right here, right now! May you be conscious of the fact you're not walking the trail alone. May you find yourself strangely lightened in spirit. May "tranquillity reign" – all is well.

PUT IT IN MY BACKPACK

OH DEAR

"BE JOYFUL ALWAYS; PRAY CONTINUALLY; GIVE THANKS IN ALL CIRCUMSTANCES, FOR THIS IS GOD'S WILL FOR YOU IN CHRIST JESUS."
1 Thessalonians 5:16–18

OUR FIRSTBORN WAS A LITTLE LATE in talking. Of course, with a firstborn you never know when they should say their first word, but as a mum I was poised with pen and paper placed in various strategic places to record the momentous occasion. Some of my friends' little girls seemed to chatter away as soon as they tipped upright and staggered around the room with squeals of delight. Not so my little boy. "Oh dear!"

"Of course, Lord," I said (with a little touch of humour), "It could be because the poor little thing can't get a word in edgeways!"

I was a little disturbed when He didn't respond to that comment but just smiled, so I put my concern aside and got on with my worried motherhood.

At long last the child spoke! I mean real words. Yes, *words* – and not just the usual one but *two* of them!

My husband worked a little way up the road. I threw the

toddler in the pram and rushed up the road to tell him our news! Bursting into his office, I announced triumphantly, "He just said something! Oh, I'm so excited. Aren't you excited?"

My man looked dutifully excited and asked, with interest, "What did he say?"

"He said *two* words," I said proudly. "*Two words!* He said *'Oh dear!'* "

As I heard myself telling the great glad news to everyone in the office the import dawned! And how embarrassing. Here was a full-time Christian youth worker reporting a dark secret. She was a worrier.

"Now I wonder where he heard *that?*" my husband asked mildly. That didn't help!

Just where *had* David heard those two little words for as long as he had been in our home. I knew, my husband knew, the staff now knew and just how many more people in my life knew?

And it wasn't just the words themselves, but the tone in which they were clearly enunciated. It was as I explained later that day to the Lord, "Like – well – like *'Oh-h-h de-e-e-ear!'*"

So from the moment my son David uttered his first sad utterance, I have been conscious of my *'Oh dear'* response to life. Yes, I am a worrier!

"If you got prizes for worrying, I'd win the biggest." I commented gloomily to the Lord. "Do you think it has something to do with growing up during the Second World War and having bombs dropped all over my life?" Then tentatively (I

FAITH DANCING

didn't want to make Him feel bad), "Or, er, did you just give me a melancholic personality so I just can't help it?"

I hoped He'd say "yes". Then I could sort of blame Him and be able to worry my life away without worrying about it!

"Whatever personality I gave you," He replied, "belonging to me should make a difference." Bother! Why did I bring it up!

"Of course," I said sounding penitential, "I know that."

Maybe, I thought, I should look in His Word and find some of His golden words to help me. I knew there were lots of them, like pressed flowers in between the leaves.

Sitting on the Steps of my Soul, I turned to Matthew 6:34, where Jesus says to His disciples "Do not worry", and I began to read. "*Oh dear*," I said to myself! "I don't know if this is going to help! I'll probably get really convicted and ashamed all over again." And then I read Thessalonians 5:16, where Paul told Christians to "be joyful, always, pray continually, give thanks in all circumstances, for *this is the will of God for you*".

Now I was in a worse fix. I glanced at the Lord. Lately, I had been having a lot of conversations with Him about what I was supposed to be doing with my life. What was His will? Should I teach in Sunday School or help with the youth work at our small church in the village where we lived? Should I invite my next-door neighbour to a Bible study or visit the sick in the hospitals with the visitation team?

Somehow, I thought, the will of God was surely about

what I was to *do*. Like speaking at meetings and teaching, singing in the choir and things.

"It's also about what *you are to be*," He said. As usual, He read my thoughts before I could articulate them. "And of course," He continued, "what you're not to be."

"Like a worrier?"

"If you really want to do my will," He replied, "and you're always telling me that you do, then *don't worry!* That is my will for you!"

"Do I have to stop doing all the other things then? Stop being so busy at church?"

"No, those activities are my will for you, too. It just depends on you doing them – worried or not!"

I determined somehow to start to be obedient. "*Oh dea–*" I began, and stopped! Something had to be done, that was evident. Not only for little David's sake, but my husband's sake, my friends' sake, but most of all for His! What sort of example was this?

"For *your* sake, too, Jill," He added quietly.

And so we sat together in the dawn of a new day and I handed the Golden Book to Him. Taking it from me, He turned to another place and read some of His priceless words.

My spirit listened. My soul smiled at the worry and it ran away! It has to, you know, when you start to be obedient and stop worrying.

Lord, there is certainly enough in our fallen world to worry about. But you have commanded me to stop. "Oh dear"! I don't know how. Lord, help me.

See me here, worrying my life away. How can this be your will? Forgive me for not trusting you with my legitimate cares. My spirit will start to listen to your helping words of peace. Bless me here, Lord; bless me – now.

Thank you,

Amen

OH DEAR

NOTHING'S CHANGED BUT ME

"YOUR EARS WILL HEAR A VOICE BEHIND YOU, SAYING,
'THIS IS THE WAY; WALK IN IT.'"
Isaiah 30:21

WHAT HAPPENS WHEN YOU WALK out of the door and into your day? Will you walk in His way? Do you make sure you're ready for whatever happens? Will you handle yourself well, as becomes a child of the King? Will you bless the people God brings your way in marketplace, home, or church? Will they wonder why they felt the breath of God as you silently prayed for them in passing? Will you encourage a friend, give a book, make a phone call or pray with someone today? Will you weep with those who weep? Or will you be carrying your personal "heart concerns" with you, becoming so absorbed that you see no one, speak to no one, touch no one, bless no one?

Do you sleep restlessly, subconsciously convinced that the big bad wolf is crouching outside "day's door", waiting for you? Do you have a devotional time before you venture forth? If you do, do you ever wonder to yourself, "Why did I bother to do that? That was a waste of time. What good did it do? Nothing's changed!"

One night, before a busy and what promised to be a difficult day, I determined to get up early in the morning and pray for these pressing personal needs. At the end of my time on the Steps of my Soul, I put all my heart concerns at the foot of the cross, opened the door of my day and walked out. The proverbial wolf growled. I knew it!

At that moment I heard a voice behind me (it's always unmistakable) saying, "This is the way; walk in it." Then, "So, Jill, while I'm working with the

NOTHING'S CHANGED BUT ME

things you just left in *my hands*, what are the things that you will be working with that I have left in *your hands*?"

I stopped dead in my tracks for as soon as the door of my day had closed behind me, I was already worrying about the very things I had risen early to talk to Him about! How silly. And how could I tell Him I would need all my energy to worry about *my* things that day and didn't think I'd have much time left over to think about anyone else's problems! Of course, I didn't have to tell Him anything!

"What would it feel like," I thought, "if I walked *free*, leaving Him to look after the things that were important to me, while I looked after the things that were important to Him? What would my day look like if I really believed He was putting His eternal mind to the problems that had been weighing me down and that I had, supposedly, left at His feet?"

That day I decided to find out: to believe. (Did I hear an angel say, "About time."?) Jesus was, I reasoned, quite capable of sorting the problems out! Now I could focus on my "day off" from running the universe! "Whew" that felt *so* good!

That night (nothing had changed but me), I was ready to sleep soundly. I couldn't wait to get up early, however late I got to sleep, and begin all over again!

Lord, whatever happens, help me to trust you with the

things I said

I trusted "You" with! Then help me to put all my heart,

mind, soul and strength,

into the things you've trusted "me" with! This is the way

— Your way, isn't it?

While I'm waiting; help me to walk in it!

Amen

NOTHING'S CHANGED BUT ME

Nothing's changed but me,
Well, not immediately!
He promised He would put His mind
To all the things I've left behind.
So why should I spend time in town
To tend to things that take me down?
Trust is the key.
While nothing's changed but me!

Nothing's changed but me,
Useless, I used to be.
I'd worry on and fuss and fret
And now, though nothing's changing yet;
The situation looks as bad –
The lost are lost, the found are sad,
And yet, I'm free!
Yes! Nothing's changed but me.

I lay my deep dark fearfulness
Down at the cross, and here profess
I'll pray, and rest, and trust my way
To Him through many a worrying day.
What liberty!
Yet nothing's changed but me!

FAITH DANCING

A PRAYER FOR A HEARING HEART

"The journey is too much for you."
1 Kings 19:7

I HAD BEEN TAKING MEETINGS far away from home, and I was reading the wonderful story of Elijah the prophet in 1 Kings 19:9–19. If you like, you could read these verses too. The verses that caught my attention were, "He [Elijah] went into a cave and spent the night. And the word of the Lord came to him… 'Go out and stand on the mountain in the presence of the Lord, for the Lord is about to pass by.'"

I then read how Elijah experienced a powerful wind, an earthquake and fire, and then came a gentle whisper, for the Lord was not in all the noise and confusion. The whisper was unmistakable and insistent. God's whisper of grace always is. And the Lord asked, "What are you doing here, Elijah?" I talked to the Lord about it.

"Elijah was so discouraged, Lord."

"He was exhausted. I cooked him breakfast," He replied.

51

"That was when he ended up under the broom tree, wasn't it?"

"Yes."

"How kind you are, Lord."

"It's not my will for my servants to retire to a cave of discouragement," He answered.

"I'm discouraged."

"I know. It's not my will that my servants are discouraged," He repeated.

"Then am I out of your will?" I asked anxiously.

There was a silent space for a moment or two.

"Lord, what am I going to do about it all?" I asked quite loudly. Then I felt bad – and almost rude. I didn't need to shout at Him, I thought. I know His ear is open to the cries of his servants.

"What did Elijah do?" He asked me.

"He went out and stood on the mountain in the presence of the Lord!" I answered.

"What did he hear?"

"Noise – loud noise. But You were not in the noise. I hear loud, frightening voices in my head, Lord, and it's hard to hear Your gentle whispers of grace above the commotion!"

"Stand on the mountain until you do," he advised. "Who are you listening to, Satan or Me?" I thought hard about that. Then I put on my coat, went a little way from where I was staying and found a hill. It wasn't a real mountain but I hoped it would do – and I stood there before the Lord.

It started to rain and I was tempted to run back to my "cave" but then I thought, "Elijah must have got wet too!" So I stayed and exulted in the rain on my face and the bending of the trees about me and nature singing a savage song. After a while the rain stopped and I heard it – *a still small voice*. I heard it distinctly, and it said something similar to what it said to Elijah thousands of years ago.

It said, "What are you doing *here*, Jill?" I knew at once what "*here*" meant. The Lord wanted to know what I was doing "in my cave of discouragement". I realized then that I had been listening to the voice of confusion and not to the voice of the Lord.

"Go back the way you came," He advised, just as He had to Elijah. "I haven't finished with you yet! There is work to do, people to talk to. There is no retirement for my children until the day dawns and they walk through my Front Door."

Then I made plans to go back the way I had come – back down the mountain of discouragement to my next assignment. Before I left I penned a prayer poem.

When storms assail and dread prevails,
when fear grips my mind,
when I'm lonely, lost, and helpless
and friends are hard to find,

FAITH DANCING

when I'm confused and desperate
I face a simple choice:
to listen to the devil
or to God's redeeming voice.

He'll whisper grace, I'll see His face,
He'll speak peace to my heart,
when doubt has wrought confusion,
and I don't know how to start
to trust again in God's great love
and the power of my King;
then I'll listen to the still small voice
till I hear the angels sing.

Lord, meet me now as low I bow
before your power and might.
Please touch my soul and make me
whole
and nerve my heart to fight.
I'll stand upon this mountain
till all my strivings cease,
and through the noise of war I hear
Your still small voice of peace.
Amen

A PRAYER FOR A HEARING HEART

Are you discouraged?

Are you hiding?

Which voice are you listening to?

"Go out and stand on the mountain

in the presence of the Lord,

for the Lord is about to pass by!"

FAITH DANCING

WAITING

"THEY THAT WAIT ON THE LORD SHALL RENEW THEIR STRENGTH."
Isaiah 40:31

SOMETIMES I GET LOST FOR WORDS. Then I borrow others. I'd love you to do the same. Be my guest!

WAITING

Fainting faith and courage waning,
Fear's grip tightens, heart stands still:
Will exhausted, Satan triumphs,
Yet a faint hope lingers still.

Body weak and undernourished,
Mind confused and dark within,
Then the breath of God blows softly,
Helps me start to hope again.

Waiting on my God and Saviour,
He who dies for sinners all,
Trusting in His mighty power,
Saviour, may I hear Your call.

Waiting, waiting, till you meet me,
Touch my heart and still my mind:
You are gentle, saving, giving,
You are love, and you are kind!

Lord, I wait for You. I will wait till You come to me.

Where else would I go for help! There is no other!

Amen

FAITH DANCING

USING WHAT'S AGAINST YOU
TO WORK FOR YOU

"THEY WILL SOAR ON WINGS LIKE EAGLES…"
Isaiah 40:31b

━━━━━━━━━━ ✦ ━━━━━━━━━━

T WAS SITTING ON A BENCH INSIDE the gate of the Garden of Grace watching a great eagle flying as only a great eagle can. He who said: "consider the birds," came near and watched it with me.

"Great Lord of eagles," I said, "just look at it, mounting up above all the things that keep us poor creatures anchored to this rude earth."

"They use the thermals: the winds of your world," He

USING WHAT'S AGAINST YOU TO WORK FOR YOU

answered quietly. "When they find themselves in the strong updrafts – they spread out their wonderful wings and soar. *They are using what's against them to work for them.* Consider the birds, Jill, and this eagle, the king of them all!"

"Look, Lord," I said, "it's not even flapping its wings!"

After that we had a lovely talk about the power of the Spirit helping the helpless to soar!

"The Spirit helps you to stop flapping and trust Him; to rest and 'rise above' with no effort or striving," He explained.

I knew I needed to soar too. And I knew He knew I knew. What was more, others expected me to soar. When you've been a Christian for a time you need to soar for all sorts of reasons. Not least, so you can show others how! So they can watch how to use what's *against* us to work *for* us.

"Like the eagle!" He said. (I love it when He does that: You know, finishes my thoughts for me!)

After watching for a while, we talked about the people in my life that the Eagle Maker was concerned about. A lot of the prayers He wants us to pray for our friends and family, and for those who don't even know the Eagle Maker yet, have to do with overcoming instead of being overcome. You know, about soaring, learning to rise above our sorrow and grief. He wants others to see how it's done just by watching us! Whoa!

I began to think of my friends. First, I thanked Him for those who were such an example to me of the "Spirit's flight". The ones who were weighed down with terrible trouble and horrible pressures, and yet were soaring.

Others, who weren't doing as well, needed to soar above chronic weariness or bleak despair. Some were trying to battle the winds of adversity, struggling to rise above impossible and even cruel circumstances. "Doing life" gets really hard sometimes! Have you noticed?

I thought of the middle-aged man I knew whose wife had died at the wheel of her car. He was left with an autistic 18-year-old who couldn't be left alone for more than twenty minutes, and he had two other children to care for as well.

All the time I was thinking about my friends, I kept my eye on that magnificent eagle – and a great joy suddenly said "hello" to my heart. Was it possible to use what was against me to work for me – the thermals of life itself? How did I begin using the hard things to lift me higher? Could I stop flapping my wings, let go, trust, and – *soar?*

"But Lord, I'm too weary even to try…" I began.

"Those who hope in the Lord will renew their strength," He replied. "Use what could destroy you to lift you up to me, Jill. Don't waste the pain, ride the winds – ride the winds."

And then He was gone and I had to decide. But it was really no contest – I was bone tired. Spiritually wrung out. I had no strength left. I edged my way into the heart of a particular storm of worry and apprehension and dared to quit using my own self-effort to fight it. My own wisdom, experience, faith, my own

USING WHAT'S AGAINST YOU TO WORK FOR YOU

"anything!" It took an effort of will to stay that still but I prayed hard and just let go, committing myself to the Maker of Eagles, men and women, the winds of this world and time and eternity! Wonder of wonders, I began to SOAR! Yes I did.

Later, much later, after I had been to Soaring School (anyone can enrol – and you'd best do it for life), I wrote a funny little poem and left it for Him inside the Garden of Grace where you can sit still and hear the praise of angels and "consider the birds". The place where we had sat together, looked up into the dark foreboding sky – and talked.

I was flapping my wings in an effort to rise
Over my troubles and all my heart cries,
When an eagle soared by me with effortless grace
While I'm flapping my wings and I'm red in the face!

I'm exhausted with flying in the face of the storm
And the blast that's against me that's causing me harm
Then an eagle above that was resting and free
Shouts, "Quit flapping your wings and ride it like me!"

Then I watched that great eagle fly up in the sky
On the Spirit's strong thermals and I heard its glad cry:
"Oh great God and Creator, I'll go with the wind
And allow all my troubles help me to ascend."

So I spread out my wings and I kept very still,
It was strange, but I sensed the sweet power of His will
Start to lift me and carry me up and above
All my troubles and tears in the power of His love.

Though tempted to flap on and help him a bit,
It so tired me out that my soul had a fit.
So I dared to let go and soar up in the sky
To "wait on the Lord" and let God lift me high!

He says, "Stop flapping your wings!"

What will you say? Say it now!

USING WHAT'S AGAINST YOU TO WORK FOR YOU

HEARING THE VOICE OF GOD

"COME NEAR ME AND LISTEN TO THIS: '… I AM THE LORD YOUR
GOD WHO TEACHES YOU WHAT IS BEST FOR YOU… IF ONLY YOU
HAD PAID ATTENTION TO MY COMMANDS,
YOUR PEACE WOULD HAVE BEEN LIKE A RIVER."
Isaiah 48:16–18

EVERYONE SEEMS TO WANT TO KNOW how to "hear the voice of God". On a past ministry trip to Egypt I had been asked that question over and over again. I was asked it by Sudanese refugees, by pastors from Upper Egypt, by ex-pats living there in business and working for the government, by teenagers from many different nations, by worried mothers, fathers, and aunts, uncles, cousins and, it seemed, by the world and his wife! It's a hot topic still. People want to know: "How do I hear His voice? What does it mean to listen to God? I want to hear Him speaking to me so how does this work? What am I listening for? How will I know it's not just a voice in my mind – my own thoughts or the devil?"

Let me share a real situation I faced a while ago. I was all hot and bothered about a problem. Some dear people had asked for help in their lives. The problem was difficult and the more they talked the more complicated it seemed to be. They were fighting all the time, hurting each other with angry words, making life miserable for their children, and were chronically anxious about everything. "We just want peace!" they said. What was at the core of it all, I wondered? Bad communication, some unfaithfulness, money issues?

"Why did you come to me?" I asked them after they had spilled out their story. "Because we think you hear the voice of God. We hoped you would pray about it for us and tell us how to fix it!" Tall order!

Well, that was fair enough. I was a Christian leader and Christian leaders were supposed to hear the voice of God. Not only for themselves but also for others. In fact, lots of people had been talking about the subject lately and having seminars and courses and writing books about it. Before they left me I prayed with them and promised I would ask God for some insight for them. Afterwards I briefly bowed my head and asked for just that, said "Amen" and went out into my busy day.

I began to work on it in my mind. I was really busy that week and couldn't see how to get any extra time to attend to their problem. I would just have to sort it out as I went along. It really began to worry me as I couldn't get it straight, and so I ran from one person to another I met in my busy ministry week, seeing if they had any ideas what to do about it (without giving names of course). They didn't! So I rushed to a Christian bookstore and hunted for a problem-solving book on marriage. It didn't help. (I even reviewed the chapter on incompatibility in the marriage book that Stuart and I had written!)

I began to lie awake at night (after a brief prayer, of course) figuring out different things to say, but my mind ran round and round and round like a hamster on a wheel and always seemed to come back to the same place of confusion.

Somewhere inside, I thought I heard a still small voice saying, *"There is something I want you to do about this — there is something you need to tell them. Why don't you ask me? I know why their marriage is struggling."* But I thought to myself I should be able to figure this one out all by myself; after all, how much marriage counselling had I done in many years of ministry? Anyway, this would require time with Him I really didn't have, as my schedule was so full speaking at conferences on prayer!

In the end, out of guilt, I got out of bed, got down on my knees and said, "Lord, do you have any advice for me?" I don't know what I expected to hear – a psychiatrist-type voice or something – but as I heard nothing at all I climbed back into bed and tried to get some sleep.

Somewhere in the early morning, between sleeping and waking, I heard a little song. I can't remember exactly how the words went, but when I woke up I got a pencil and scribbled them down as best as I could remember. The words I heard between sleeping and waking were much nicer than the words I wrote on the paper and rhymed a lot better, but I did my best. They went something like this:

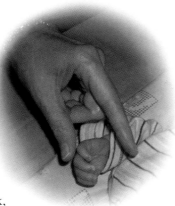

> Heart of the hurried one,
> Listen to me.
> Open your inner eyes,
> What do you see?
> Sit your soul down today,
> Hear what I have to say,
> Heart of the hurried one,
> Listen to me.
>
> Heart of the worried one,
> Come to my throne.
> Read My Words in My Book,
> Then make them known.
> Lay down your heavy care,
> More than a mind can bear,

Heart of the puzzled one,
Come to my throne.

Heart of the harried one,
Rest in my grace.
Bring your confusion,
Slow down your pace.
Take time to look above,
Revel in my quiet love,
Heart of the harried one,
Come to this place.

So that day I did without lunch, found a quiet park and just "came to that place". I couldn't see Him but somehow I sensed His presence all around me.

"Why does it take me so long to come here and let you speak to me, Lord?" I murmured. "Why do I not learn the lesson of listening for Your voice through your Word? Why do I waste time trying to get a grip on this problem and discern what is best for people in a mess any other way?" Then, "Please Lord." So we all sat down together with Him – my hurried heart, worried soul and mind and me – and wondered greatly what was going to happen.

First I listened. It was hard because I didn't know quite what I was listening for! Would I hear a voice? Would He speak in a thought? How would I know it was His voice and not just my imagination? Maybe an angel would come with a "deep knowledge pill" and I would drink it with some of the Living Water that's always available down in the lives of His own, and like magic all of me would "get it" and feel better!

But not one of these things happened. I began to get fidgety. After all, I had even missed lunch to come and hear His voice and I had a lot to get done that day. I had wasted a good half hour already listening for I knew not what!

At long last I began reading the Golden Book looking for some help and David's words from Psalm 119 were at once in my mind: "Your word is a lamp to my feet and a light for my path" and "Open my eyes that I may see wonderful things out in your law". A sense of expectation arrived on the doorstep of my confusion. I was glad to welcome it.

I was reading in Isaiah the prophet, who was speaking to worried Israel who had been disobedient inviting disaster and had been suffering the consequences of their actions. At this point in their history they were trying to understand "why" they had been allowed to suffer the results of their sad actions and were asking each other why they had no peace of mind. And as I read on, there were the very words I had heard in my song at the dawn of the day: "Come near me and listen to this…" *Come near and listen to me!*

I continued reading the prophet's message: "And now the Sovereign Lord has sent me, with His Spirit. This is what the Lord says – your Redeemer the Holy One of Israel: 'I am the

Lord your God, who teaches you what is best for you… If only you had paid attention to my commands, your peace would have been like a river.' "

The people who had come to me for help had not been paying attention to His commands and had, in fact, been living in disobedience to God for a long time. I knew this but had been trying to work with their problems arising as if they were disconnected with this disobedience! As if a disrupted and rebellious attitude to God would not have repercussions in all of their relationships. I saw it now clearly.

This was the way I heard the voice of God that day: Through His Word and applying a principle in the scriptures to the present problem. We all need to pay attention to His commands and rules. And that includes the rules of Christian marriage.

I relaxed. My mind stopped running round and round trying to figure out what was wrong at the core of things, and peace began to flow into my hot and bothered mind like a river. It was such a relief! So refreshing!

Now I could help the troubled couple to get things right with God and start living a life of obedience – and then peace would begin to flow into their troubled relationship too. Peace like a river!

Thank you, thank you, dear Lord –

I have heard your voice.

Help me to be obedient now to give your words to these

dear people who came to me for help.

Give them grace to hear and receive them.

Amen

HEARING THE VOICE OF GOD

AS USUAL

"JESUS WENT OUT AS USUAL TO THE MOUNT OF OLIVES…"
Luke 22:39

"As usual, Lord?"

"As usual."

"Like – regularly?"

"Yes, regularly."

"Like a – habit?"

"A habit."

"A serious habit?" Silence.

"Lord, aren't habits sort of legalistic? Like rules and regulations? I thought if we were your children we didn't need rules and regulations."

"Children don't need rules?"

"Well, well yes – but aren't we supposed to be free?"

"Free from what?"

"Rules and regulations!"

"Like the rule of living a disciplined life? The rule of love is a discipline to be practised. If you love me, keep my commandments."

"The commandments – like the 'usual' ones?"
"The usual ones!"
"I'm coming, Lord."
"Hurry!"
"Yes!"

A treasured moment in the dawn
When hope returns and faith is born;
A time with God, communion rare,
A place where He and I can share,
Here He reminds me of His law
And I am overcome with awe.

As usual He and I talk long
And as I leave I sing a song;
This habit practised regularly
Births strength of character in me,
Such holy habits daily done
Bring blessings from His One dear Son.

AS USUAL

EVEN WHEN

> "EVEN WHEN I'M OLD AND GREY, DO NOT FORSAKE ME, O GOD,
> TILL I DECLARE YOUR POWER TO THE NEXT GENERATION, YOUR
> MIGHT TO ALL THAT ARE TO COME."
> Psalm 71:18

Even when I'm old and grey,
Sun or rain or come what may;
Even when my strength is waning,
Help me, Lord, with knowledge gaining:
Tell the children of your grace,
Show them how to seek Your face.

Give me inner eyes to see
What you have in mind for me.
Grant me "patient power" to wait
Till I pass through heaven's gate:
Even when I'm old and grey,
Give me strength, Lord, day by day.

FAITH DANCING

Thank you for Your Spirit strong,
Deep within me all day long,
Freshening my thirsty soul,
Strengthening and making whole.
Jesus may my children see,
Your sweet life controlling me.

Even when I'm old and grey,
I'm resolved to have my say.
Even when they laugh or frown
I won't let it get me down.
Count on me to tell Your story
Till You take me home to glory!

Even when... even when... even when.

EVEN WHEN

"'THEM' IS US"

*S*TUART AND I WERE AT THE COVE – the beautiful Billy Graham centre in the North Carolina mountains. There are fabulous views all around the lodges nestled in the trees. On each terrace surrounding the halls and meeting rooms there are rocking chairs. We were there to speak to "seniors" – over four hundred and fifty of them.

"I love ministering to them." I remarked to Stuart after the first day.

"'Them' is us, Jill," he replied!

"Oh, I suppose," I answered! I never think much of my senior status. I used to have birthdays but gave them up for Lent a while ago. But I had to admit the rocking chairs looked very inviting indeed! I went to the Throne Room to talk to Him about it.

"It's strange, Lord, but I don't think about ageing when I'm here with You. Maybe it's because I'm more aware of life rather than death when we meet beneath the praise of angels." He just smiled at me.

During the three-day conference it was hard to find a rocker unoccupied. I watched the Grandmas and Grandpas rocking away and joined them whenever I got a chance. Just think about it: all those hundreds of rocking Grandmas and Grandpas!

Somehow, even with so many of us occupying the same space, it was really easy to talk to Him while I was rocking. Why

was that? I asked myself. I wondered if all my peers were having the same experience. Was it that such an occupation reminded us of our senior status? After all, when it was getting time to step through the Front Door most elderly folk find themselves in a rocking chair thinking about it.

We found out during the week that many seniors felt marginalized by their churches, and frightened by world events. They told us they felt somewhat helpless to influence their children and children's children in such a frightening world. They seemed to be rocking their way to heaven to a sad rhythm of seeming irrelevance.

"Lord," I began one morning, "this is sad. Most of these sweet folk have a measure of health, or so it seems. They have more discretionary time, more money and hopefully wisdom and experience gained to be making a huge impact for You, but they feel, rightly or wrongly, ignored by their fellowships. Is it because of the huge emphasis on the youth culture?"

" 'Them' is us," He said with a smile, reminding me of my husband's comment.

"OK," I began again, "we have all this to give – so why doesn't the church put us to work?"

"You didn't wait for the church to ask you," He replied. "You just got going and kept on keeping on."

"True," I said. And I realized that Stuart and I viewed this stage of our life as "Grand Time". And what was more, the best was yet to be. Our 70s had been the most productive time of our lives, I think – I hope! Yet we were eyeing our 80s with no less enthusiasm than we had viewed our 70s!

After the conference ended, Stuart and I said goodbye for a few days as we went our separate ways to speak at different events. While sitting on a wonderful white rocker (of which there are dozens at Charlotte airport – is this a conspiracy or something?) waiting for my connection, I decided I would not rock my way to irrelevance for the rest of my Grand Time, but would ask the Lord to make me a Grandma to be reckoned with *for Him*! I wrote the prayer down, as is my habit, so my grandkids could look ahead with "grand" anticipation to their Grand Time too! I called it "Rocking Grandma".

> Rocking on for Jesus,
> Rocking round the world,
> Rocking on for Kingdom truth –
> The gospel flag unfurled.
> Rocking on for Jesus,
> Not planning to retire,
> Rocking on for Jesus
> Until the final hour.
>
> Grandma has a passion
> And a vision for the lost,
> A mission light within her eyes
> Regardless of the cost.
> So Grandma goes a-rocking
> To tell her world she's His,
> And it doesn't really matter
> That she doesn't know where she is.
>
> Lost on every continent,
> Confused in lands afar,
> Kind and noble policemen come
> To help her find her car.

And when she loses many things
Like passports, keys and pen,
Kind folk mysteriously appear
And, find them all again.

Rocking round the garden,
Rocking round the gym,
Rocking round the shopping mall,
Keeping svelte and trim.
Rocking, rocking, rocking,
Keeping up with things,
Determined to expand her brain
Untill she gets her wings.

Rocking with the grandkids
Whenever she gets the chance,
Reminding them of what they know:
The heavenbound upward glance.
Reminding them of Jesus
If they want her to or not,
For this is "Rocking Grandma" –
The only one they've got!

Coming to the Throne Room
A hundred times a day,
My heart so loving grandkids,

FAITH DANCING

I'm lost for words to say,
Jesus listens carefully
To hopes and dreams and pain,
Then He calls to God His Father
"Grandma's come again!"

The Father listens carefully
And looks for spirit meek,
Then bends in blessing and I feel
His kiss upon my cheek!
I come right from the Throne Room
And journey back through space,
Praying that my grandkids see
His heaven on my face.

So, if the rocking grandkids
Respond to what's been sown,
So when they're rocking gently
With grandkids of their own:
They'll see their generation
Love the Father and the Son,
And through the Holy Spirit
They'll pass the faith right on.

Jill Briscoe, age 71

EVERLAND

There is a place that you can go
Where fears and phobias laid low
Retreat before His power and might
And darkness flees before the light.
There is a place so near at hand,
Called Everland.

There is a Presence waiting there
Who'll heal the hurt and life-despair,
You simply enter through a prayer,
To Everland.

Is there a peace you long to gain?
A hope of joy replacing pain?
The Spirit's balm to heal your soul
The Master's touch to make you whole?
It's what He's planned
For Everland.

So one day robed in "glory dress",
The fitting clothes for Everness,
We'll look like Jesus; home at last
Our guilt and shame will all be past,
So take His hand
To Everland.

FAITH DANCING

Lord, here I am in rags of sin,

Please cleanse my heart and enter in.

Amen

EVERLAND

CHRISTMAS GRACE

"FOR YOU KNOW THE GRACE OF OUR LORD JESUS CHRIST, THAT
THOUGH HE WAS RICH
YET FOR YOUR SAKES HE BECAME POOR, SO THAT YOU THROUGH
HIS POVERTY MIGHT BECOME RICH."

2 Corinthians 8:9

Grace abounding, sin confounding,
Heaven has come this morn!
Death defeating, Satan beating,
Jesus Christ is born!

Grace abounding, men astounding,
Jesus born today.
Grace embracing all we're facing,
Help us, come what may.

Grace o'erflowing, men not knowing
Christmas in their soul,
Help me tell the great good news that
Christ can make them whole.

Lord, you are full of grace.
You give us what we don't deserve!
You gave us Jesus! Hallelujah.
Amen

CHRISTMAS GRACE

JOY IS JESUS

Joy is Jesus wrapped in swathing bands,
Joy is Jesus in Mary's loving hands.
Joy is Jesus making sorrow sing,
Mending deepest heartaches – what a gift to bring!

For from the highest heavens knowing well His plan,
God laid Him in our hostile hands, the precious Son of man.
And knowing all before Him – the crib, the cross, the cost –
He came to die at Calvary and seek and save the lost.
That's you and me and everyone who's living on this earth,
That's men and women, black and white, who need a second birth,
That's those of us with broken hearts and those who celebrate,
It's those who love and laugh a lot, and those of us who hate.

If empty was the manger and empty was the cross,
If Jesus' tomb was occupied, then all of us are lost.
But here lies heaven's treasure, God's precious, dearest prize,
In Him will all our future hopes and dreams be realized.
So may His joy now fill you and the peace of God be known
Till we celebrate our Christ-masses together round His throne.

KNEELING WITH KINGS

" 'WHERE IS THE ONE WHO HAS BEEN BORN KING OF THE JEWS? WE
SAW HIS STAR IN THE EAST AND HAVE COME TO WORSHIP HIM.' "
Matthew 2:2

Kneeling with kings in Christ's cattle stall
Shepherds, the innkeeper, commoners all,
Kings in their glory have come from afar
Led there by a miracle star.

In the deepening darkness and shadows of sin
Man coming short of what man should have been
The plan of redemption begun for the race
Lighting our lost-ness with grace!

Kneeling and praising
Adoring and gazing
Forgive my transgressions
Lord, hear my confessions
My will now submitting
My life here committing –
I'm kneeling with Kings, with Kings.

Lord, I'm reaching for heaven while fastened to earth,
Invited to glory through the gift of His birth
My words without language are carried above,
As I kneel and am lost in His love.

Candlelight flickering, light on His face,
Gift of the Lord God, a baby of grace
With my heart on its knees and tears in my eyes,
Here may You hear my praise rise.

My soul softly singing joins in the refrain
Of angels' sweet music as praise heals my pain,
Worshipping here, my heart near Your throne
Kneeling and knowing I'm known!

Kneeling and praising
Adoring and gazing
Forgive my transgressions,
Lord, hear my confessions.
My will now submitting
My life here committing –
I'm kneeling with Kings, with Kings!

FAITH DANCING

CHRISTMAS WITHOUT WINTER

"GLORY TO GOD IN THE HIGHEST, AND ON EARTH PEACE TO MEN
ON WHOM HIS FAVOUR RESTS."

Luke 2:14

*C*HRISTMAS! ETERNITY WRAPPED in a baby, ever a mystery – a miracle of grace. But how to keep the focus? As we rummage through boxes, silver paper and tinsel trivialities, looking for Bethlehem, how do we miss the shepherds, kings, sheep and angels? What happened to us? Have we, to use C.S. Lewis' words, become practised at celebrating "winter without Christmas?"

For the first eighteen years of my life, Christmas was a party in the middle of hard winter. It seemed a good idea. An excuse for a "fun and games" family reunion in our beautiful English home in Liverpool. Rummaging through some old pictures I took my photographs to The Steps of my Soul and showed Him what I had found.

"Very nice," He said.

"It's a long time ago," I said. "Over fifty years or more! Pretty nostalgic."

"In my land there is no 'long time ago'," He said.

FAITH DANCING

"It will be strange," I said.

"You'll like it," He replied.

"Then if you don't wait till the season comes around like we do down here, Lord, do you just keep the decorations up all year long?"

"Wait and see," He said with a smile.

Now it was yet another Christmas in my world – another year. But how to keep the focus? It seemed as hard to find Jesus in the wrapping paper today as it had been all those years ago! As I shared the old photos of my family at our Christmas gathering with Him, He reminded me that this was my very first real Christmas.

He didn't mean my first as a baby, but my first as a baby Christian, for I had been born again when I was eighteen years old at in the winter term at college. We talked about what had happened when I went home after my conversion for my first "Christmas without winter". And I remembered.

"Even now, Lord, I can almost smell the chestnuts roasting on the fire, and hear the soothing voice of my dad's favourite artist, Bing Crosby, crooning, 'I'm Dreaming of a White Christmas!' "

I could see in my mind's eye the games we would play as the extended family gathered at our house. I remembered the faces of the guests who would come and go, bringing fruit cake, nuts and mince pies, and the rousing music enjoyed each night around my father's electric organ.

The organ was as near as we got to tipping our hat in God's direction. It was not that we sang carols, but pretty Rudolph and "sleigh bells jingling" songs, and ditties about "decking the halls with holly". It was a wonderful winter celebration, but "a winter without Christmas". Happy hoopla, yes, but Christ's-mass? No!

"Lord," I said softly, "we threw a big bash for years but never invited the guest of honour. I'm so sorry!"

"You made up for it, Jill," He said cheerfully. "Remember?"

How could I forget! I had travelled back from Cambridge by train, my mind racing to 25 December. What would I do that I had never done? What wouldn't I do? I didn't know, so I went through some mind scenes practising my lines!

"Mother and Dad, why don't we invite Jesus to 'His' party this year?" No that would be too much! "Let's sing a carol instead of Rudolph?" No, they wouldn't want to do that unless it was "Holy Night" and we didn't know the words. We didn't go to church.

Once home my struggle intensified. I scanned the newspaper for a local church service to go to on Christmas Eve. And I found one – at midnight! Public transport would stop at 12 a.m. and I would need to walk home. I decided I was going anyway.

"It was miles away, remember, Lord?"

"I remember." He had been watching as I slipped out of the house with the level of the songs rising as the Christmas "cheer" began to talk.

An hour later, I found the little chapel crammed with people in the soft candlelight. Smiling eyes full of wonder, love and praise greeted me. Jesus was here. We sang at the top of our lungs, hearts bursting with thanksgiving for "Divinity wrapped in a blanket in the shape of a man child". He who had come to earth to bring us back from the dead was as present with us then as He was now, as He sat on the Steps of my Soul and we remembered together.

That night, in that small chapel in Liverpool, we Jesus lovers prayed and smiled knowingly at one another. Total strangers bonded together by a belief in the Christ of God who came to take away the sin of the world. He knew we needed eternal life and there was no other way to bring it to us but by the way of a crib and a cross. We were in awe at "Christmas Grace". It was my first Christmas without winter. Heaven. I didn't want it to end. But it did.

The walk home took over an hour. It took me past homes lit with a holiday glow, the wafting aroma of chestnuts, the sound of the lusty singing of songs, and the chiming laughter of family togetherness – the like of which was waiting for me. I slowed my steps wanting to sing all the carols I knew (very few) one more time at the top of my lungs, telling my Liverpool world what the Lord had come to do.

On the doorstep I could hear things "revving up". I slipped into the crowd as unobtrusively as I could but my mother's friend saw me.

"Why, here she is," she announced, louder than I wished. "We didn't know where you were."

"She's been to church," my sister said.

"How do you know?" asked the friend.

"Look at her face," my sister answered softly.

Eyes turned my way. There was a sudden quieting. I went pink! What were they looking at? My cheeks were surely tingling with the cold but something else seemed to be catching their attention.

"Apparently they saw You, Lord," I said. "I'm so glad."

"Then you were content," He reminded me.

"Yes Lord. They knew I was changed for ever."

My mind returned to that Christmas long past. Another day I would try and explain it all to my family. Now it was time to slip up to my mother and father and my beloved sister, give them a kiss and wish them from the bottom of my heart a "Christmas without winter"!

CHRISTMAS WITHOUT WINTER

Father, we pray for our families that they may know 'the

Peace Child Jesus" and in knowing him to be blessed

beyond measure, enriched beyond their wildest dreams.

Amen

DOWN IN MY LIFE

"I WANT TO KNOW CHRIST AND THE POWER OF HIS
RESURRECTION..."
Philippians 3:10

T IS NEW YEAR'S DAY. As I look out across another year with all its known and unknown challenges, I remind myself that what transpires for God and for good as far as my small life is concerned, depends on what happens "down in my life". How do I go deeper, reach further, climb higher, cling closer, dream bigger, and be seen to be empowered by the Spirit, in touch with the risen Christ, with an unmistakably evident relationship with the Father – deep down in my life? In other words, what does it mean to live in the present reality of the living God?

I know there is absolutely no way I can do the work I've committed to do on the "outside" of me, unless God is doing the work He has committed to do on the "inside" of me. I simply need to give Him permission to be who He is, as "deep down" as He wishes to go! This is my prayer not only for me, but also for you my friends.

Down in my life where it's restless and wild,
Down in my life where the adult's a child,
Down in my fears and worries and care,
Suddenly Jesus is there.
Touching my heart strings He sings me a song,
Quiets the child till she's steady and strong,
Banishes worries – just smiles them away,
Turning my night into day.

Down in my life where the troubles run deep,
Down in my life when I can't get to sleep,
Down in my life when life isn't fair,
Suddenly Jesus is there.
Rebuking the turmoil He sends it away,
Gives peace in the panic and helps me to pray,
Turns sorrow to praising, surprises my pain,
And bids me to face life again.

Down in my life where I'm lonely and old,
Deep in my heart when my spirit is cold,
Down in my life when I don't know what's best,
Suddenly Jesus gives rest.
"Gift doesn't age," He remarks with a smile,
"I'll set your soul dancing and make life worthwhile,
I'll guide you in righteousness: wisdom's delight,
And nerve your faint heart for the fight."

FAITH DANCING

He stands in my shadows and the light on His face,
Reflects all His love and His mercy and grace,
Right down in my life where nobody goes,
Deep in "this" heart the Lord knows.
Down in my life where it's restless and wild,
Down in my life where the adult's a child,
Down in my soul I'm acutely aware –
Suddenly Jesus is there!

Pray this prayer with me:

Dear Lord, hear my heart. I give You full permission to

be who You want to be, as "deep down" as You wish to

go!

This is my prayer not only for myself, but also for my

family and friends.

Amen

DOWN IN MY LIFE

A LIGHTNESS OF SPIRIT

A lightness of spirit
A touch of His grace,
Lifts a weight off my shoulders
Puts a smile on my face.
The prayers of Your people
Are felt in my heart,
And Your blessings enfold me
As they do their part.

Will you thank them for me, Lord,
Will You bless them today,
For you've prompted Your people
To kneel and to pray.
Will you fill with Your Spirit
Again and again,
And return them the favour
As I pray for them!

LOOKING

"Sometimes, Lord, I don't know where to start when we get together. Help me, Lord."

He sat down on the Steps with me and told me it wasn't really hard.

I wrote down what He told me. It helped! I hope it helps you too.

Help me, Lord, to look *above me*,
Show me things that I can tell,
From the heavens that will capture
How You manage all things well.

Help me, Lord, to look *within me*,
Seeing how You've made me whole,
Help me craft this into stories
That will help win people's souls.

Help me, Lord, to look *about me*,
Ever eager to impress
God's good gospel on the listener,
Telling them of Ever-ness!

WHERE DID I LEAVE MY LIFE?

Where did I leave my life? I'd put it down somewhere and couldn't remember where. I am always doing that with my glasses, or a book that I'm reading, my purse, watch, and pens. But this time I didn't know where I'd left my life!

Stuart was a bank inspector before he laid down his career and went to work in youth work. While he was inspecting banks he would always look for documents the bank employees had mislaid by saying first of all, "It will be somewhere with something on top of it!" I thought about that. That could possibly be true where life is concerned.

Have you ever felt as if you have put your life down somewhere and mislaid it? Maybe someone else, or even life itself, put something on top of it! Perhaps you were in business, got married and had three kids. You put your life down into marriage and motherhood. A few years later, after hectic early child-rearing years, and it seems that all your friends are finishing their Master's degrees and working in corporate America. Do you feel you mislaid something? This may lead you to ask yourself, "Where did I leave my life?" "It will be somewhere with something on top of it," the Lord will say. Start lifting things! Look underneath child rearing, or a long period of ill health, or hurt, betrayal, or disappointment.

At times I have looked for my life under such layers of stuff.

WHERE DID I LEAVE MY LIFE?

Sometimes I found it under a pile of busy care-giving or even neglect of my spiritual disciplines. At others, domestic duties, bread-winning, or obscurity made me wonder where life was.

Say to Him, "Lord, where did I leave my life?" He will help you to look for it. Rediscover life as he intended it to be at whatever stage. *With* whatever has been "laid on top of you". Whatever the "something on top of you" is, don't allow it to blind you to the fact that the Lord appoints each day with all its challenges. I believe God appoints me and my appointments, layering His tasks on my life as He sees fit. Our job is not to lose our perspective in the differing seasons of life.

Whenever this feeling of "missing something" happens to me, I spend time with Him asking, "Where did I put my life?" I realize He has my times in His hands and knows "the good works, which God prepared in advance for us to do". Many times He has helped me to see disappointments and seemingly wasted years as His appointments, coming from His nail-pierced hands.

If you find yourself in this position, ask Him to help you see all of life's "layers" as permitted things and live life as it is *for* Him. Remember, he or she that "loses their life for His sake will find it". Pray:

Appoint these things in Your own good time and in Your

matchless way as You see fit, dear Lord.

Amen

RETURNING THE FAVOUR

A lightness of spirit
A touch of His grace,
Lifts a weight off my shoulders
Puts a smile on my face.
The prayers of Your people
Are felt in my heart,
And Your blessings enfold me
As they do their part.

Will You thank them for me, Lord?
Will You bless them today?
As You've prompted Your people
To kneel and to pray,
Will You fill with Your Spirit
Again and again?
And return them the favour
As I pray for them!

WHERE DID I LEAVE MY LIFE

SURPRISE

"THINKING HE WAS THE GARDENER, SHE SAID, 'SIR, IF YOU HAVE
CARRIED HIM AWAY, TELL ME WHERE YOU HAVE PUT HIM, AND I
WILL GET HIM.'
JESUS SAID TO HER 'MARY.' "
John 20:15, 16

SHE CAME BY DAY TO BURY HIM. She knew no fear when she had known the company of demons. She only feared existence without Jesus. Her day was night, her world a world of tears. She watched Him on the cross and missed not one tortured movement, neither word, nor forgiving prayer. She watched Him die; tormented by the demons He had cast out of her. Her Jesus! And now she sought His body and found it not – as if He never was. As if it were a dream. As if He never touched her, healed her, loved her, and compelled her to lay down her sin. Then suddenly the "gardener" was there, right in front of her.

Poor Mary! She knew He was dead; she'd watched Him
die,

SURPRISE

Hanging between the earth and sky.
She knew He was dead; she'd heard Him scream.
As the filth of our sin had come in between,
Himself and His God, as the punishment rod
Fell to chastise His choicest prize.
She knew He was dead, so pardon her
For thinking Him only the gardener!

He called her name; He was just the same,
Save the holes in His hands and His spear-pierced frame.
The love and fire in His eyes were too much,
The strength and the thrill of His risen-life touch.
Dear Lord! Dear Lord! Oh, pardon her
For thinking you only the gardener!

Many folks that I know have a Jesus of gloom,
Alive, yet confined to His garden tomb.
Yes, He came alive, but was never the same,
He never called them by their very own name!
He lives in His tomb and He tends His grave,
Confined and helpless to seek and to save.

Look into His face, let go of His feet,
Stop trying to wrap Him in that winding sheet!
He isn't the gardener, a ghost, or a fake,
He's Rabboni, your Master and He rose for your sake.

FAITH DANCING

Lord God, in the power of the

resurrection surprise us

in our pain.

Wipe the tears from our eyes

as we discover you

in our garden of grief.

You are risen indeed!

Amen

SURPRISE

GOOD TO GO

*B*EFORE I GOT ON ONE MORE PLANE to go to one more place, I stopped at Starbucks. After I got my order, I asked if it was a latte, and the girl said, "Yes, ma'am, *you're good to go.*" She meant that I had received what I'd ordered – I was now supplied with the zap of energy I needed. At the airport they wanted to look though my bag again. (I wondered why I didn't just wear a bathing suit and wrap to go through security.) After the long check was over, the official said, "There you are, *you're good to go!*" She meant I had all the right things on my body and in my bags.

I was on the way to a prison. When I'd told my granddaughter where I was going, she asked anxiously, "Is that legal, Nana?" I had laughed and replied, "Oh, I'm not going to prison like a prisoner, sweetheart; I'm going to talk to hundreds of prisoners about Jesus." She had looked very relieved and promised to pray for me. You can't buy that!

Every year at about this time, I join a team of volunteers from Discipleship Unlimited who work in the Texas prisons. They train volunteers from churches and pull together a "crusade" for

GOOD TO GO

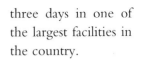

three days in one of the largest facilities in the country.

My assignment was to speak in five chapels, pray with the prisoners when allowed, and in a few places we had been given permission to actually put our hands on them and hug them (only the women of course!). Some of the team goes cell to cell and some to death row.

Our dear friends, Linda and Dallas Strom, have worked officially in this huge federal complex for years. Dallas has been battling cancer and last year the team said goodbye to him! A year later, in God's grace he is still with us – but barely. Now in hospice care he was able to come to say goodbye (again) to his team and many of his closest friends.

Speaking with tears and difficulty from Acts 20 – Paul's farewell to the Ephesian elders – I waited for the verse I knew he was heading towards.

Paul, addressing his beloved brothers and leaders of the church said, "Now I know that none of you among whom I have gone about preaching the kingdom will ever see me again."

GOOD TO GO

Oh my! We – the team – and some of Dallas and Linda's close friends felt we were on the shore with Paul and the Ephesians. I looked at this giant of a man (not only physically, but spiritually) and thanked God, both for the privilege of knowing him and also for this moment. What an honour to be instructed by a man of God, who, as Spurgeon said, "was sitting in the suburbs of the new Jerusalem".

Afterwards, I said my farewell personally and he assured me with a big smile that he was *"good to go!"* There was no question about that! He asked me to tell his much-loved men in the men's unit that he couldn't come and teach them that night, but had asked me to thank them for their love, prayers and tears, to say that he loved them dearly and that those who knew Jesus should be sure to follow on to know and love the Lord. This was my assignment. When I asked what he suggested I taught, he told me "to feed them" as they had not had chapel for months. "God will tell you," he added. "They are so hungry!'

What the team can do in the different prisons depends entirely on the authorities of the particular unit. Last year – my first time in this particular unit – I was thrilled to hear the prisoners' own worship team leading the singing, and admired the beautiful Jesus mural they themselves had painted on the wall. There was also a library stocked with Christian books and Bibles. Alpha courses (Bible studies exploring the Christian faith) were being run led by local church teams, and men were committing their lives to the Lord every week.

When Dallas came to chapel he was able to teach and pray with the men, and when he told them he had had a serious setback medically they asked the guards to allow them to leave their seats and pray over him. The guards assented. The scenes were amazing and were repeated in the women's prisons.

But this time it was very different. There had been a "changing of the guard" – the mural had been painted over, the band disbanded, and the Christian library was nowhere in sight. No chapel services had been allowed for months. The night before the "crusade" the team had a long prayer meeting about it. The next day the governor, who was very supportive of the work Dallas and Linda were doing, called to tell Linda that they could send a speaker *and* a band to the men's unit! The team was *"good to go"*.

"But Lord, who is sufficient for these things?" I asked anxiously as we arrived at the unit and began the long process needed to go inside. "And what do I teach for one and a half hours? 'No small groups allowed. No interaction with prisoners.'"

Sitting on the platform watching the chapel fill up as the men were ushered in, I panicked. I thought back to last year. What had I taught? I couldn't remember! What if I taught the same thing? That would be embarrassing! Oh, if only I knew I could follow on. I sat very still as the band continued the worship songs and I watched the men longing to stand up to praise the Lord (not allowed), lift their arms or fall to their knees in their places (allowed). My heart ached. "Stand up on the inside," I told them wordlessly. "He will see you!"

"Lord, I need to know what I did last year," I prayed desperately. I didn't know why but somewhere deep down in my life I thought if I knew it would give me my cue. In fact, I somehow was certain it would. But how could I remember? How many hundreds of messages had I used between then and now?

Suddenly, my attention was caught by a guard talking to a Hispanic man near the back. He was pointing to me and gave the guard something. The guard walked round the seats, came up on the platform and handed me the man's Bible. It was large, dog-eared and well scribbled all over. I looked up and the man gave a wonderful big smile and pointed upwards! "He wants you to sign it," the guard said briefly.

I turned to the front page and there, neatly written and concisely arranged, were full notes of my teaching the year before! I looked up and mouthed to my brother in the Lord, "Thank you – you'll never know!" For, reading the notes, I knew exactly what I needed to do.

Ten minutes later I was on my feet thinking, "An hour and a half, Lord? I have no notes with me. You know how I need notes!"

"It will not be long enough," I heard Him say. And then, *"YOU'RE GOOD TO GO!"* What more did I need but His Spirit?

I told them the story of King David. The five smooth stones

– the building blocks that made that kid a giant-killer before the age of twenty. Moving on to the episode of Bathsheba, I talked about temptation and the steps up to the roof. How laziness and laxness in David's spiritual disciplines led to disobedience, and so on. I didn't let Bathsheba off the hook either. They appreciated that! She was lonely and she was bored and her husband was out of town! David didn't get off the roof and neither did she! Havoc.

Then we turned to Psalm 51 and spent the rest of the hour walking through David's psalm of repentance with its triumphant climax. All sin is "big sin". There is no sin too big for God to forgive. And there *is* life after sin. Even though David, a man after God's own heart, broke seven of the Ten Commandments in one night of lust, he finished up saying "a broken and contrite heart... You will not despise" and "I will teach transgressors Your ways, and sinners will turn back to You". We finished with a long prayer time. I led from the front and looking out I will not soon forget the picture.

As the men were walked back to their cells, my Hispanic friend (who had been diligently writing in his Bible the entire time) looked up at me and mouthed, "Thank you, Mother!" His smile wouldn't quit. He was *"good to go"*.

> *"I pray, Lord, for all in prison that they may find the*
>
> *freedom of forgiveness.*
>
> *And I pray for all who seek to visit, bless and pray.*
>
> *Strengthen us to be*
>
> *'good to go' there and do the loving and caring, the*
>
> *listening and learning,*
>
> *the crying and the praying."*

Deep down in my heart I think I heard Him say, "Hurry back, there is a lot of work to do!"

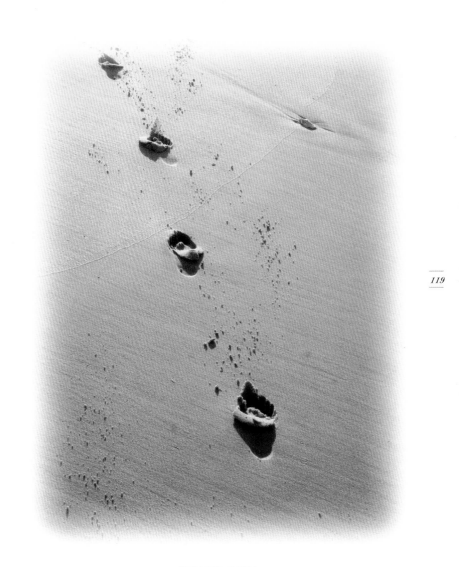

THANK YOU

THANK YOU

Thank you for the will to praise
My Father God through all my days;
Blessings more than I can name,
For, first and foremost, Christ who came,
Saving, changing, lifting high,
Those who weep, and hurt and sigh.

Thank you, God, for hearts that sing,
Thank you, God, for everything!

Thank you for the chance to love
A God who lives in heaven above.
Thank you for a world to tell
About the One who saves from hell,
Thank you, Lord, for trusting me
With serving, giving ministry.

Thank you, God, for hearts that sing,
Thank you, God, for everything.

Thank you, thank you, for the day
When hard-won freedom came to stay,
Giving us a chance to grow

FAITH DANCING

And better serve our God below.
Forbid we take for granted here
The things that cost our fathers dear.

Hear my heart, its anthem sing,
Thank you, God, for everything!

"Thank you for thanking me," He said with a smile. "Never take your freedom to freely worship for granted."

"Oh, I won't, dear Lord," I replied.

"Always remember what your freedom is for," he continued seriously.

"Freedom to —?" I paused, thinking hard. What was the freedom our fathers had fought and died for all about?

"It's not freedom to 'do what you like'," He reminded me. "It's freedom to 'be what you ought'. Never forget it!"

"I'll try not to," I promised.

Then I prayed for all the people in other countries who had little or no freedom of religion. How blessed we are.

"Help us to use our freedom for Your 'kingdom things', Lord," I prayed.

Why don't you ask Him to help you to do the same?

THANK YOU

When you've been blessed with a partnership that has lasted fifty years, it's easy to take each other for granted. Don't do it! I was reminded of this one day when I read this piece of writing from Stuart.

I JUST WANTED TO BE WITH YOU!

WHEN THE CHICAGO CUBS COME to play the Milwaukee Brewers, Miller Park is usually packed to the rafters. As tickets are hard to come by I never pay my annual visit to watch the Brewers on such an occasion. However, a couple of days ago a business man friend casually handed me a packet of tickets to a Cubs–Brewers game, and on examination I discovered they allowed access to a luxury suite with seats for twenty people *and* front row parking! He explained that he couldn't attend the game and hoped I could round up my kids and grandkids and take them for a night out! So began a fast and furious few hours of phone calls which resulted in an impressive gathering of eighteen Briscoes and in-laws – including my wife Jill.

Architecture

I JUST WANTED TO BE WITH YOU.

After the game – which the Cubs won, to the delight of our Chicago-based family members – I teased my wife about the fact that she had found time, despite leaving for England the next morning, to come to the game with us and suggested, rather ungallantly, that it was amazing what influence the grandkids wielded! To my surprise – and shame! – she replied quietly, "An old friend called me this week to say her husband had just died. She told me, 'Jill, don't assume you'll always have each other. You won't. So never miss an opportunity to spend time together.' You see, I just wanted to be with you. That's why I came." Winston Churchill was once asked if he had ever regretted saying something. He replied, "On occasion I have been required to eat my words but I have found them delectable!" Mine stuck in my throat!

Jill and I have always lived busy lives and our ministry over the years has, at times, necessitated long absences. When our children were young I was regularly called away for ministry overseas for three-month periods. And since stepping down from pastoring to minister in the developing world we have been known to say "Goodbye" at Bangkok airport as Jill flies to Croatia and I head for Cambodia. It's no surprise then, that our book on marriage was originally published under the title, *Pulling Together When You're Pulled Apart*.

I'm not complaining, neither is Jill. We were called to ministry and ministry involves sacrifice. This was what we were required and privileged to do. And we have done it – and still do it – with joy. But it has not always been conducive to "time together". Perhaps Jill's friend, knowing this, was prompted to give her those words of advice. Maybe, looking at our 48 years together, she suspected we're a little like those Pennsylvanian Dutch who are "Too late smart".

But on reflection I have concluded that the issue was not simply that our calling required us to be separate some of the time. It's not easy to be together apart! I was also aware that when we were together, that is when we were in the same geographical location at the same time, we were often so busy that we didn't have time to be together. I know that, before her friend called, if I had asked Jill if she wanted to come to the ballgame (knowing that she was leaving for England the next morning), the answer would have been, "I can't – I have to pack and finish a writing assignment." And, in similar circumstances, my response to her suggestion that we might go out for dinner would have been, "Can't we grab a bite at home? It will be much quicker."

I JUST WANTED TO BE WITH YOU!

"Much quicker," of course, is a dead give-away. "Grab a bite" speaks volumes too. Taking time to eat a leisurely meal in pleasant surroundings while actually talking and listening to each other *takes too much time!* Consume food but don't consume time. But what is time for? Surely it is a fleeting, infinitely precious gift in short supply that is granted to earthlings in order that they might invest it in the mystery of living? And people are designed to live in the realm of the relational, and there is no relationship more significant than the one that exists between two people who through the wonderful purposes and power of God have been made one.

When Jill spoke those simple words "I just wanted to be with you", I realized how much I wanted to be with her. Even if it meant being together in a noisy stadium, packed with 35,000 rambunctious fans in a suite full of lively grandkids – at least we could catch each other's eye in the constant movement and share an unspoken thought across the proverbial crowded room. And the drive home that started with us trying to escape the stadium parking lot – which took forever – was not a frustration. It was time together.

When I said that under normal circumstances Jill might have declined the invitation to go to the ballgame using the "excuse" that she had to pack, I was speaking the truth. She actually did leave for England the next day. And it was the day that Scotland Yard, MI5 and the Pakistani Intelligence Service cracked the plot to blow up airliners bound from London to the USA, creating consternation and chaos in London just as she arrived! I was watching the breaking news of this horrendous "attempt at mass murder on an unprecedented scale" and wondering where she was when the phone rang. Caller I.D. informed me it was my pal Jim Scheel. (Jim volunteered years ago to drive us anywhere we needed to go, which has meant endless trips in all weathers from Milwaukee to O'Hare and back. He said it was part of his ministry.) With my mind full of terrorist plots and my wife somewhere on the other side of the Atlantic in the middle of the chaos, I picked up the phone and said, "Hi Jim, how're you

I JUST WANTED TO BE WITH YOU!

doing?" The voice answered, "This isn't Jim. He died a couple of hours ago."

I rushed over to Jim's home to be with Ina, his widow. She greeted me, incredibly, with the words, "You lost your ride." But my mind was not on rides. It was focused on a brave little lady who was suddenly living with the harsh reality that we don't always have each other! She told me how the Spirit of God had brought to her mind the words, "Be still and know that I am God" even as she tried to resuscitate Jim's lifeless body. "I *was* still in my heart, for I know that God is God." We prayed, relatives began to arrive and as I drove away from the house of mourning, my international cell phone rang. It was Jill! From London. She was fine and had spent the day recording and speaking live on the Premier Radio station from which we broadcast to our homeland every day. "How are you?" she asked. "I'm hurting. My buddy Jim Scheel died." Sensing my sorrow she replied, "I'm so sorry Stu." Then she added, "I wish I could be with you."

I cried when I read this again. Then I prayed:

"Lord, thank you for the years you have given
us to be together in heart, mind and purpose if
not always in body.
No regrets, Lord – help us both to make every
moment count when we are privileged to occupy
the same small space on this little swinging
planet.
You know. You come first."

Jill

"I know I do. I will make every moment count.
I love you. Be blessed in your love for me and for
each other. See how I will enlarge your hearts.
See how I will bless your love."

Jesus

AUTUMN LOVE

Written on the occasion of a widow and widower's marriage.

The Artist lays His brush down – and smiles.
His painting is finished. He calls it... "Autumn Love".

This Autumn Love, painted with
Spring colours, framed in faith,
hangs in God's gallery.
We look, we gaze, we are as
much surprised by joy
as you!

Autumn Love – the same beloved trees,
yet now
bedecked with such new dress,
it startles us with its new life.
A man united with his wife!

Autumn Love, basking in a
warm September,
thankful for the summers past –
with precious partners,
loved by both in equal measure,
yet finding now a present treasure:
new and lasting love.

Autumn Love, fearing not the winter's coming,
having now the other's hand to hold!
Savouring now this vibrant season,
suddenly, with bright new reason to exist –
and love again.

Autumn Love, mature in matching grief,
and with great grace determined more
to look into His face than e'er before.
We watch you walking through the open door
of sacrificial service
waiting for you both.

Autumn Love, only One such Artist
paints like this.
We see His signature
Agape.
We laugh, we cry, we know the reason why,
He paints His pictures on the canvas of your lives.
And so we too like you, would spend our days in endless
      praise.

Autumn Love!

A "FIGHT FOR LIFE" FLIGHT

"God is not unjust; He will not forget your work and the love you have shown Him as you have helped His people and continue to help them."

Hebrews 6:10

═══════════ ⟲ ═══════════

On a plane flight I found myself sitting next to an "unaccompanied minor". It caused me to listen carefully to one more flight attendant giving one more safety talk telling us that if the plane got into difficulties, oxygen masks would drop down and that I the adult would need to assist the child to acquire life-saving oxygen. Thinking about it, I realised suddenly that this would be really hard to do, especially if the child was panicking: obviously in distress and looking to me for help. My instinct would be to grab the mask and fit it quickly over the child's face first, before attaching my own.

That day as I listened with more attention than usual to the stewardess, I realized if I was breathing in a steady steam of

FAITH DANCING

life-giving air in order to stay alive, I would have the best chance to help!

My mind went to the people around the globe who were in crisis situations. Especially the children. Those who were "unaccompanied" by adults who cared. Those in crisis situations in a world in deep, deep trouble. There were those in the West: children of divorce flying across the country between parents (as was this child) feeling at times strangely "alone" among strangers. Then there were the children in the East, India – our next port of call. The Dalits: the "untouchables" of the caste system who were enslaved by it.

Stuart and I and a team from our church were setting off soon to help. Yes, a "drop in the bucket", I know. But if more people would add their drop perhaps the bucket would fill up. I knew from previous experience that this month's ministry ahead of us in India: the travel conditions, the heat and dirt, the heartbreaking sights, the people gasping for the breath of life itself, would affect us all deeply and engender an immediate response from us.

But you know, first – day by daily day – I knew we must breathe deeply of the Spirit's air ourselves. We must do what it takes each day to fill our spiritual lungs so that we can stay alert to rescue and encourage, comfort and instruct, listen and pray with those we find ourselves sitting next to.

The Dalits of India are dehumanized, discriminated against, exploited, enslaved and oppressed. All this through poverty,

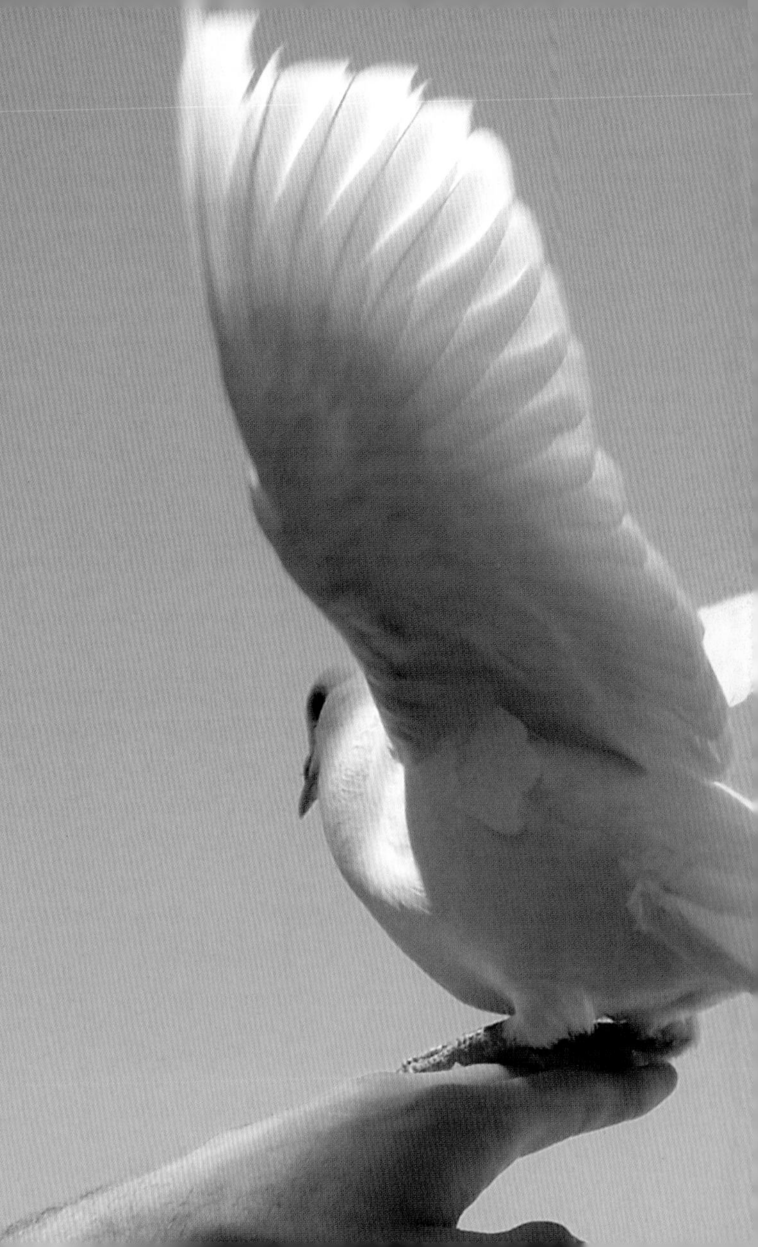

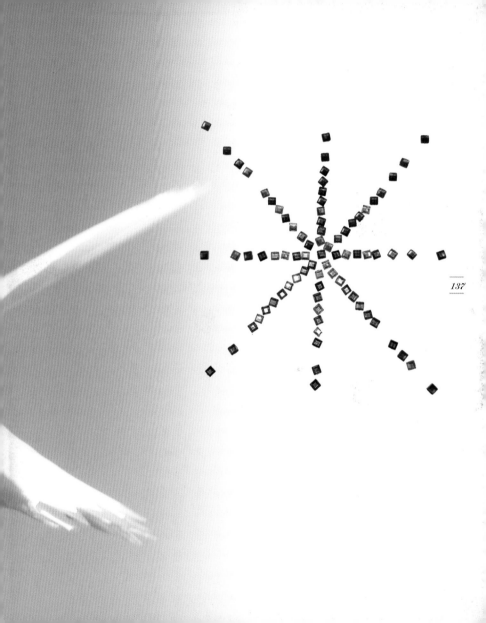

illiteracy, segregation, persecution and violence. Human Rights Watch revealed 100,000 atrocities against Dalits in 2006. Every two and a half hours a child under 13 is raped. Every 13 hours a child under ten is raped. More than one million children are missing in India today, largely because of the sex trafficking industry.

What a privilege in this emergency situation to be sitting for a short "flight" in the "next seat" to these children at such a time as this. I thanked God for all of God's pastors and leaders in India and, indeed, around the world: some engaged in schools work, right there among the squalor, or church planting, health work, small business ventures or involved in the training of Indian leaders. Informed prayer is essential on the home front and, as we boarded our "fight for life" flight, I knew we could bank on it. I penned a prayer for the team and settled down to support our missionaries waiting for us.

Breath of life, the Spirit's power,
Mercy given for this hour,
Coursing through my heart and mind,
Giving words for lost mankind.
Breathe o'er me that I may breathe
Life that lost ones may believe.

Breath of life, the Spirit's love,
Breathe upon us from above,
Daring not to use our own

We come to plead before Your throne.
Breathe o'er me that I may breathe
Life that small ones may receive.

Breath of Life, the Spirit's hope,
Strengthening my heart to cope,
Ready me to take Your light
Where your children live in night.
Breathe o'er me that I may breathe
Life for hurting ones that grieve.

Breath of life, the Spirit's peace,
Breaking bonds, giving release.
Gracing those You died to save,
Promised rescue from the grave.
Breathe on me that I may breathe
Truth so lost ones will believe.

Breath of life, the Spirit's joy,
Use me now, my tongue employ.
Hands and feet and heart are given
Spend me for the cause of heaven.
Breathe on me that I may breathe
Life that lost ones will receive.

Jill Briscoe, 2008

Jill is author of *God's Front Door, The Deep Place Where Nobody Goes, The Garden of Grace* and *Prayer that Works*. In total, she has authored more than forty books, including devotionals, study guides, poetry and children's books. Her vivid, relational teaching style touches the emotions and stirs the heart. She serves as Executive Editor of *Just Between Us*, a magazine of encouragement for ministry wives and women in leadership, and served on the board of World Relief and Christianity Today, Inc., for over twenty years.

Jill and her husband Stuart call suburban Milwaukee, Wisconsin their home. When they are not travelling, they spend time with their three children, David, Judy and Peter, and thirteen grandchildren.

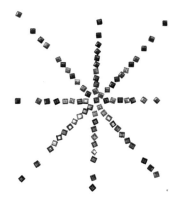